P9-DME-262

STEM *trailblazer* BIOS

SUPER SOAKER INVENTOR
LONNIE JOHNSON

HEATHER E. SCHWARTZ

Lerner Publications ◆ Minneapolis

Lerner Publications Company
A division of Lerner Publishing Group, Inc.
241 First Avenue North
Minneapolis, MN 55401 USA

For reading levels and more information, look up this title at www.lernerbooks.com.

Content Consultant: James A. Flaten, Associate Director, NASA's Minnesota Space Grant Consortium

Library of Congress Cataloging-in-Publication Data

Names: Schwartz, Heather E., author.
Title: Super Soaker inventor Lonnie Johnson / by Heather E. Schwartz.
Description: Minneapolis : Lerner Publications, [2017] | Series: STEM trailblazer bios | Includes bibliographical references and index.
Identifiers: LCCN 2016044353 (print) | LCCN 2016046906 (ebook) | ISBN 9781512434477 (lb : alk. paper) | ISBN 9781512456325 (pb : alk. paper) | ISBN 9781512450996 (eb pdf)
Subjects: LCSH: Johnson, Lonnie, 1949–—Juvenile literature. | African American inventors—Alabama—Biography—Juvenile literature. | Inventors—United States—Biography—Juvenile literature. | African Americans—Alabama—Biography—Juvenile literature.
Classification: LCC T40.J585 S39 2017 (print) | LCC T40.J585 (ebook) | DDC 338.7/68872 [B] — dc23

LC record available at https://lccn.loc.gov/2016044353

Manufactured in the United States of America
3-45730-25390-5/4/2018

The images in this book are used with the permission of: © Thomas S. England/LIFE Images Collection/Getty Images, pp. 4, 28; Mouse in the House/Alamy Stock Photo, p. 5; Per Andersen/Alamy Stock Photo, p. 6; PhotoStock-Israel/Alamy Stock Photo, p. 8; AP Photo/John Bazemore, p. 10; © Silver Screen Collection/Moviepix/Getty Images, p. 11; NASA, pp. 14, 15; Jim Zuckerman/Alamy Stock Photo, p. 17; © Grey Villet/The LIFE Picture Collection/Getty Images, p. 18; JOE ROSSI/KRT/Newscom, p. 20; © iStockphoto.com/modzelm1, p. 21; Ken Love /Akron Beacon Journal/Newscom, p. 23; AP Photo/Atlanta Journal-Constitution/Jessica McGowan, p. 24; Chris Zuppa/ZUMAPRESS/Newscom, p. 25; © foxbat/Shutterstock.com, p. 26.

Cover: © Thomas S. England/The LIFE Images Collection/Getty Images.

Main body text set in Adrianna Regular 13/22. Typeface provided by Chank.

CONTENTS

Chapter 1

Lonnie Johnson shoots water from a Super Soaker water gun.

FEARLESS
INVENTOR

Growing up, Lonnie Johnson showed plenty of promise as an inventor. He took things apart and built his own creations. He experimented, made mistakes, and moved forward with new ideas. Anyone could see he was smart, creative, and motivated.

But not everyone in his life expected him to succeed in a big way. Lonnie was a black student in the **segregated** South and did not have much opportunity. Despite these challenges, he became a US Air Force and National Aeronautics and Space Administration (NASA) engineer. He also invented the Super Soaker, one of the most popular toys in the world.

The Super Soaker is a super high-powered water gun.

ALABAMA CHILDHOOD

Lonnie was born in Mobile, Alabama, on October 6, 1949. He was the third of six children. His family was far from wealthy. But they were hardworking and handy. Lonnie's father, a driver for the military, taught Lonnie to make his own toys. They once made a berry shooter together out of bamboo. A smaller piece of bamboo was used as a plunger, and a larger one was used as a tube. Sliding the plunger inside the tube created air pressure that launched the berries into the air.

A street in Mobile, Alabama, Lonnie's hometown

Lonnie got more creative as he got older. He also took bigger risks. One time, he built a go-kart from junkyard scraps. He even built an engine for it. When he tested it out along the highway, police pulled him over. Another time, Lonnie decided to make homemade rocket fuel in his kitchen. The fuel exploded and started a dangerous house fire.

His parents were supportive, though. They let him try again. When Lonnie got his recipe right, he used the fuel to launch a small rocket for a school project.

SEGREGATED SOCIETY

The rest of Lonnie's world was not so supportive. He lived in the South at a time when black people and white people were legally segregated in public places. Even schools were segregated by race. White students had advantages that black students didn't have. Schools for white students had more money and better equipment.

Segregated buildings had separate doors for white and black people to use.

SEGREGATION STANDOFF

In 1963, the University of Alabama was the site of a standoff in the movement to end segregation. Alabama governor George Wallace stood in a doorway to prevent two black students from enrolling in the all-white school. The National Guard stepped in to make him move and allow the students in.

Lonnie attended Williamson High School, which was for black students only. He had always had big ideas. But he was advised against pursuing big dreams for his future. He was discouraged from becoming a scientist. He took a test that seemed to suggest he didn't have what it took to become an engineer either.

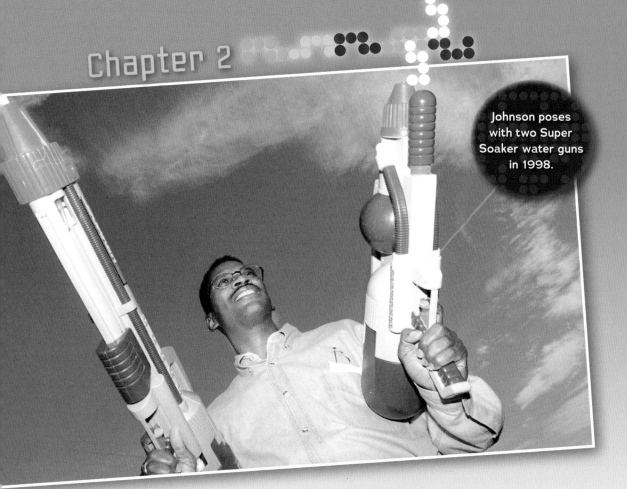

Chapter 2

Johnson poses with two Super Soaker water guns in 1998.

CAPTURING
ATTENTION

Lonnie didn't let other people's **prejudices** get in his way. He dreamed big despite the obstacles he faced. He kept moving forward with his ideas. His intelligence and inventions earned him a nickname from his neighborhood pals. They called him the Professor.

BUILDING A DREAM

During his senior year of high school, Lonnie was inspired by one particular goal. He wanted to build a robot. He wanted it to work like the robots he saw on a popular TV show called *Lost in Space*. But there was one important detail he didn't understand. The robots on the show weren't real. They were actors wearing robot costumes.

In *Lost in Space*, a spaceship goes off course when its robot is reprogrammed.

Lonnie worked all year to build his robot. He experimented with materials. Police stopped him when they spotted him riding his bike and carrying sheet metal. He didn't get in trouble when he explained his project.

Lonnie created a 3.5-foot-tall (1-meter) remote-controlled robot. He made its "brain" from a tape recorder and walkie-talkie parts. He created a system of frequencies and tones that signaled the robot to move. The robot's torso was made of a propane tank filled with compressed air. The air moved the robot's arms, and it rolled around on wheels. Lonnie named his robot Linex.

AN INSPIRATION

Learning about inventor George Washington Carver inspired Lonnie to succeed in science. Carver was born a slave around 1864. He grew up free after the Civil War (1861–1865). He fought for his education. He is most famous for inventing hundreds of products made of peanuts, including fuel, soap, and cheese.

A WINNING PROJECT

In 1968, Lonnie entered a state science fair. It was held at the University of Alabama. He was the only black student with a project in the fair. He also represented the only black high school there.

The university was known for prejudice against black students. But the science fair judges were not part of the college—and they were impressed. Lonnie and Linex won first prize.

Lonnie was a little surprised that the university didn't ask him to attend the school. He was an intelligent and creative student. He had proven himself at the fair. He might have attended the University of Alabama after high school.

Instead, after graduating from high school, Lonnie went to Tuskegee University, a historically black college in Tuskegee, Alabama. He received a **scholarship** from the US Air Force and another one for his skills in math. And even though he was told in high school that he would never become an engineer, he earned his bachelor's degree in mechanical engineering. Then he earned his master's degree in nuclear engineering. His education prepared him for a bright future.

Chapter 3

Johnson began studying space launches such as this one in 1975. His work impressed NASA.

SUPERIOR SOAKER

fter college, Johnson worked in the Air Force Weapons Laboratory for the Space Nuclear Power Safety Section. He studied space launches and the use of nuclear power in space. He uncovered a technical problem that it seemed NASA had missed. He was rewarded with an invitation from NASA to work on the Galileo mission in 1979.

The goal of this mission was to send an unmanned spacecraft to Jupiter and its moons. Johnson's job involved supplying the spacecraft with electricity from a small nuclear power source called an RTG (radioisotope thermoelectric generator). He enjoyed solving technical problems to make sure power reached the spacecraft's systems, including its computer, scientific instruments, and power controls. He designed a system to protect the power supplied to the spacecraft's computer memory, even if other parts of the power system failed.

An artist's image shows NASA's *Galileo* spacecraft flying past Jupiter's moon.

Johnson worked on other space missions too. He helped send spacecraft into space to study Mars and Saturn. His job was exciting. But he never stopped tinkering in his spare time.

ACCIDENTAL DISCOVERY

In 1982, Johnson spent his off-hours experimenting with a new kind of heat pump. Most heat pumps used a substance called Freon to cool air. But Freon is bad for the environment because it damages the ozone layer of the atmosphere. The ozone layer protects Earth's surface against ultraviolet light.

Johnson wanted to develop a heat pump that used water instead of Freon. He built a **prototype**, and one night, he attached a part of the pump to his bathroom sink. He was shocked and delighted when a stream of water shot across the room into his bathtub. The surprising accident immediately gave him an idea. He wanted to invent a new type of toy water gun. Other water guns used a trigger pump. The trigger pushed a small piston into a cylinder filled with water. They couldn't shoot much water at once, and they couldn't shoot very far. Johnson wanted his water gun to be more powerful.

PERFECTING THE PRODUCT

Soon after, Johnson started a new job back with the US Air Force. He began working on the stealth bomber program, which developed aircraft that could fly undetected by radar. Months passed, but he finally got back to his water gun idea.

He built a prototype from plastic pipes, a plastic Coke bottle, and plexiglass. He used tools to cut and carve the parts he needed. Then he put it all together as a pressurized toy water gun. The gun used a pumping mechanism to pump air into the water tank. The water was under so much pressure that it shot out in a powerful blast.

By then, Johnson had a family, including his seven-year-old daughter, Aneka. He let her take the prototype outside and test it with her friends. The other kids' squirt guns were no match for his invention.

Johnson's toy gun worked. But he could see it wasn't perfect. He tinkered tirelessly to get the design just right. He also had to figure out how to mass-produce the toy so he could sell it. Years passed, but he kept working and learning. He kept showing the toy to people who might be able to help.

Johnson's water gun was much more powerful than the small water pistols available when he was growing up.

Sometimes he showed it off just for fun. One day, he brought his invention to an air force picnic. He demonstrated the toy by shooting an officer between the eyes. The other picnickers threw cups of water, and a spontaneous water fight broke out.

Chapter 4

An early
version of the
Super Soaker
water gun

SUPER SOAKER
SUCCESS

Johnson faced many challenges. But he believed in his new toy—and himself. He left the air force to start an engineering company. He called his business Johnson Research & Development.

In 1989, he took his toy water gun to the American International Toy Fair in New York City. Buyers and sellers of toys could connect at the fair. Johnson made a good connection. He met someone from the Larami Corporation. Al Davis, the company's vice president, told Johnson he was interested in the toy. But he needed to see it at Larami's headquarters in Philadelphia.

AIMING HIGH

Johnson went home and got to work. He wanted to make his toy even better. He used plexiglass, a soda bottle, and plastic pipe to create a new prototype. He changed the design. He moved the bottle from inside the gun and placed it on top. This allowed him to use a larger bottle that contained even more water.

Johnson's prototype water gun used a plastic soda bottle as the water tank.

After a few weeks, he was ready to bring it to Philadelphia. In a meeting with Larami executives, he shot blasts of water in the meeting room. He aimed for some coffee cups and shot them off the table. The Larami executives loved it!

Larami bought Johnson's invention. The company wanted to sell it. But first, Johnson had to put in even more work on the design. He needed to make the gun less expensive to manufacture. That way, Larami could sell it for $10 and make a **profit**. The $10 price tag was meant to be affordable for **consumers**. But it was still high compared to the price of other toy water guns.

Larami started selling the Power Drencher in 1990. It was soon renamed the Super Soaker. Johnson also redesigned it once again. He created a system that pumped water into the gun instead of air. The earlier model got more difficult to pump as pressure built up. The new model used two bottles to prevent that from happening. It was much easier for children to pump. In 1991, Johnson's invention earned $200 million in sales. It was the best-selling toy in America.

Super Soakers quickly became a favorite water gun for kids in the United States.

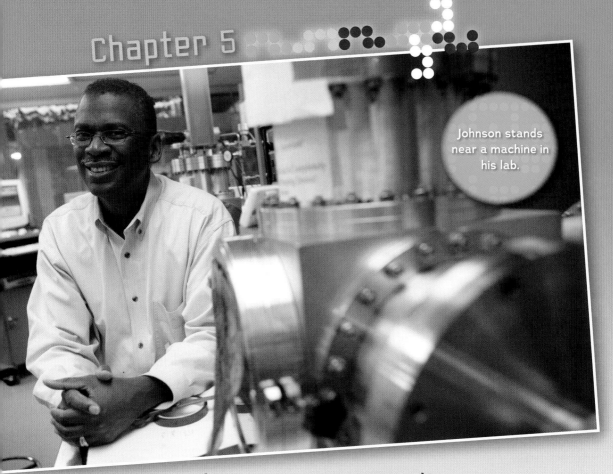

Chapter 5

Johnson stands near a machine in his lab.

FORWARD THINKER

Johnson earned **royalties** from the sales of his Super Soaker. He put most of his money back into his company. There, he could continue doing the work he loved. He designed many different Super Soaker models. He worked on other inventions too.

One of Johnson's inventions was a water-based cooling system called the Johnson Tube. He created it for NASA. It was more efficient than an air conditioner. He also designed more toys. One was a Nerf dart gun that operated on air pressure. He invented a diaper that plays a nursery rhyme when it's dirty. He invented hair rollers that don't require heat.

A Nerf dart gun

Johnson's work on toys wasn't just about creating fun products. Designing the Super Soaker and the Nerf gun helped him explore his scientific ideas. He began studying other science that interested him, such as battery technology and electrochemistry. Eventually he invented a more efficient rechargeable battery. He also invented the Johnson Thermoelectric Energy Converter (JTEC). The JTEC converts solar energy into electricity. It is more efficient than other systems. It's also more environmentally friendly.

Like many others, Johnson values clean energy and wants his products to be environmentally friendly.

TECH TALK

"Some of the problems that I see today are problems that I experienced when I was a kid in the segregated South growing up. Somehow we need to have a fundamental change. I think technology will provide us a tool to use to bring about that change. But the change is a social change; it's a community change. It's an attitude change."

—*Lonnie Johnson*

Johnson holds eighty **patents** on different inventions. He has twenty more pending.

In 2011, Johnson was inducted into the State of Alabama Engineering Hall of Fame. He continues to work at his lab. For him, the work is about more than inventing new products. It's about making change. His company has created new jobs, and it employs many people. Johnson also encourages young people interested in science.

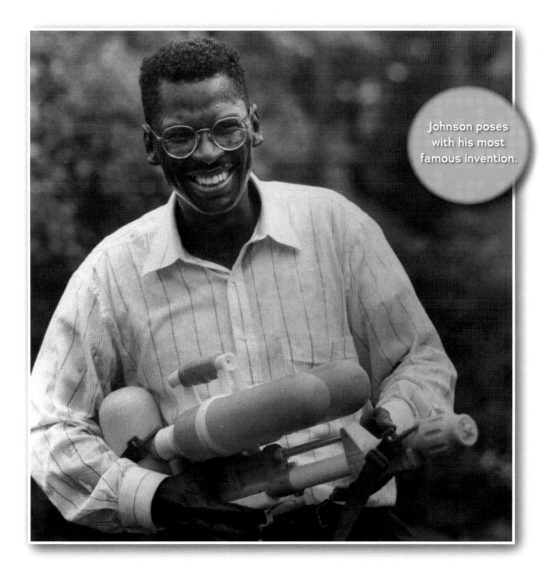

Johnson poses with his most famous invention.

The inventions developed at Johnson's lab are meant to change the world for the better. They make the world more efficient and environmentally friendly. And they make it more fun too!

TIMELINE

1949
Lonnie Johnson is born.

1963
Alabama governor George Wallace prevents black students from registering at the University of Alabama in a bid to support segregation.

1968
Lonnie wins first prize at a state science fair held at the University of Alabama.

1973
Johnson receives a bachelor's degree in mechanical engineering from Tuskegee University.

1975
Johnson graduates from Tuskegee University with a master's degree in nuclear engineering.

1979
Johnson begins working on the Galileo mission for NASA.

1982
Johnson creates the first prototype for the Super Soaker.

1989
The Larami Corporation buys Johnson's Super Soaker and begins to sell it. Johnson starts his own company, Johnson Research & Development.

1991
The Super Soaker earns $200 million in sales and is the most popular toy in America.

2011
Johnson is inducted into the State of Alabama Engineering Hall of Fame.

SOURCE NOTES

7 "Lonnie Johnson: The Father of the Super Soaker," *BBC News*, August 15, 2016, http://www.bbc.com/news/magazine-37062579.

19 Ibid.

22 William J. Broad, "Engineer at Play: Lonnie Johnson; Rocket Science, Served Up Soggy," *New York Times*, July 31, 2001, http://www.nytimes.com/2001/07/31 /science/engineer-at-play-lonnie-johnson-rocket-science-served-up-soggy .html?_r=0.

27 Candace Wheeler, "Super Soaker Inventor Now Engineers Batteries at Atlanta Lab," *WABE 90.1*, July 16, 2015, http://news.wabe.org/post/super -soaker-inventor-now-engineers-batteries-atlanta-lab.

GLOSSARY

consumers
people who buy goods and services

patents
documents that give people or companies the right to be the only one to make or sell a product for a period of time

prejudices
unfair feelings of dislike for a person or group because of race, religion, or other characteristics

profit
money made by a business after costs and expenses

prototype
the first model of a new product

royalties
money paid to the original inventor of a product based on how many are sold

scholarship
an amount of money given by a school or organization to help pay for a student's education

segregated
separated by race

FURTHER INFORMATION

BOOKS

Abdul-Jabbar, Kareem. *What Color Is My World? The Lost History of African-American Inventors*. Somerville, MA: Candlewick, 2012. Learn about other black inventors.

Barton, Chris. *Whoosh! Lonnie Johnson's Super-Soaking Stream of Inventions*. Watertown, MA: Charlesbridge, 2016. Read more about Johnson's life as an inventor.

Jacobson, Ryan. *Exciting Entertainment Inventions*. Minneapolis: Lerner Publications, 2014. Find out the stories behind some incredible inventions that you use every day!

Wulffson, Don. *Toys! Amazing Stories behind Some Great Inventions*. New York: Square Fish, 2014. Explore how some of the world's most popular toys came to be.

WEBSITES

How I Made My Millions
https://www.youtube.com/watch?v=HpvEF_Glhmw
Hear Johnson talk about inventing the Super Soaker.

Time for Kids: **Famous Inventors**
http://www.timeforkids.com/homework-helper/study-helper /famous-inventors#next
Take a quiz that asks who invented what. Do you know who invented the chocolate chip cookie?

INDEX

ABOUT THE AUTHOR

Heather E. Schwartz has written more than sixty nonfiction books for kids. She always enjoys researching and learning about people with a passion for what they do, such as Lonnie Johnson.